THE
CADILLAC POEMS
OF
Steven Forris Kimbrough
(1958-2010)

THE
CADILLAC POEMS
OF
Steven Forris Kimbrough
(1958-2010)

Introduced by S T Kimbrough, Jr.

ARCHWAY PUBLISHING

Archway Publishing books may be ordered through booksellers or by contacting:

Archway Publishing
1663 Liberty Drive
Bloomington, IN 47403
www.archwaypublishing.com
1-(888)-242-5904

Because of the dynamic nature of the Internet, any web addresses or
links contained in this book may have changed since publication and
may no longer be valid. The views expressed in this work are solely those
of the author and do not necessarily reflect the views of the publisher,
and the publisher hereby disclaims any responsibility for them.

Any people depicted in stock imagery provided by Thinkstock are models,
and such images are being used for illustrative purposes only.
Certain stock imagery © Thinkstock.

ISBN: 978-1-4808-1278-9 (sc)
ISBN: 978-1-4808-1279-6 (e)

Library of Congress Control Number: 2014919255

Print information available on the last page.

Archway Publishing rev. date: 03/16/2015

This book of poetry is dedicated to Dakotah Starr Kimbrough
and Savannah Rain Kimbrough, the children of
Steven Forris Kimbrough, who often inspired
the images, thoughts, and eloquent diction
that enrich their father's poetry.

Contents

Odes to Love

Odes to the "I"

Odes to Self

Odes to Faith

Miscellaneous Poems

Preface

The Poems of Steven Forris Kimbrough

THESE ARE THE POEMS of a man who died tragically young. They are poems of a life lived to the full, and experienced in all its pain and all its glory, the glory that comes from living in touch with the things that really matter: love and its loss, friendship, happiness and unhappiness, nature, health and sickness, the whole business of an authentic life. These poems hold within themselves the emotional pressure of a life of feeling, in the sense that they express states of mind that many of us would seek to avoid, as well those which we can share and rejoice in. They are poems of the soul, not in any conventional or pious way, but in their openness to many kinds of experience. They are moral without being judgmental, for their morality is based on a shared and sensitive humanity.

Steven Kimbrough knew what he was writing about. His hospital poems are reflective and accurate, and his love poems are full of the roller-coaster demands of relationship and commitment. The nature poems are the result of an acute ear and eye, part of the engagement with felt life that marks these poems at every point. It is life without fear and without hesitation, precious in its everyday experience, precious too in its stand for truth and honesty. Nothing is hidden here, and nothing is excused. The result is a poetry that lingers in the mind as powerfully as wood smoke, or the sight of the first snowdrops in spring, or the sound of a cadence of music, heard in the heart long after the music has stopped.

I commend these poems to all who believe, as I do, in the

power of poetry to give form to the hopes and longings of human experience, and to all who find, in that form, a heightened perception of life itself.

Richard Watson
Emeritus Professor of English,
University of Durham, Durham, UK

Introduction

BEFORE THE WRECKER TOWED the old 1992 Cadillac to the junk-yard, I thought perhaps I should open the trunk to see whether anything of value had been left there. I hailed the driver, and he stopped. He handed me the key, and I placed it gingerly in the lock. When I turned it, the trunk sprang open with a pop. A stifling, musty stench arose from a frame of mildew surrounding a shiny metal footlocker in the middle of the trunk well. When I grasped the handles on both ends and attempted to lift it, I realized that it was much heavier than I had imagined. The driver of the wrecker helped me lift it and carry it into a nearby shed. I wondered, *What could possibly be so heavy?* Once the locker was safely situated on the floor, I lifted the top as though there might be some hidden treasure within. I was not disappointed. Amid a plethora of books and thickly packed file folders, I found three journal-like volumes filled with handwritten poems by my son, Steven, who had died three months earlier. The old Cadillac, one of his three cars, had not been driven for a number of years and was parked near a shed on his three acres of land in the rural community of Cedar Grove, NC. He had loved to drive the Caddy and just couldn't part with it, though it was no longer operable. As I discovered, it became one of his many storage spaces.

As the executor of his estate, I had the responsibility of going through his belongings, all of which had been inherited by his two teenage children, Dakotah and Savannah. On his property there were numerous sheds surrounding the old farmhouse adjacent to which lay a beautiful pond trimmed by exquisite pine, oak, gum, and maple trees. And of course, there was the old

Cadillac, which opened to me a treasury of Steven's verse that I would soon call *The Cadillac Poems*.

☙❧

Steven Forris Kimbrough, fifty-one years old, *magna cum laude* graduate of Duke University, graphic artist, poet, and father of two, died in an automobile accident on January 5, 2010. He had just picked up his son, Dakotah, from school, who was seated in the front of the car opposite his father, who was driving. Savannah was in the backseat. As they entered a familiar intersection, Dakotah screamed as he saw a silver-colored car fast approaching. It was too late. His father was struck directly on the driver's side. Dakotah blacked out briefly and awakened to his father's body slumped over his own. Savannah had managed to phone her mother but was extremely distressed and passed the telephone to Dakotah. The mother asked, "What just happened?"

He replied, "We were in a car wreck. I think Ate (a Native American word for father) is dead." And so it was. At the scene of the accident Steven was declared dead with a severed spinal cord.

He had often said to me that he would probably be the first of four brothers to die. He was never morbid about death, and as a lover of words and the craft of writing, he would have deeply appreciated the eloquent essay Dakotah wrote for his high school English class about the accident and his father's death. Here are just two of the moving paragraphs:

> Friday at the funeral home, my thirteen-year old cousin Mattie was my only cousin there. She had come all the way from Texas with her part of the family. That meant a lot to me. Though our first meeting was only last November, in that moment we both felt as if we'd known each other our whole lives. I hobbled over on crutches to meet her, as my legs had been injured. In the viewing room, as I looked upon my father's face, my uncle

Timothy took me and my sister by the shoulder and said, "There's Brother Steven. He is your father, and he is not." My aunt helped me cut a lock of my father's long, dark, graying hair.

I lost my best friend that fateful day for he was the only person that truly knew me, and I fear that I will never have a connection like that with anyone ever again. But my family was there for me, and what a great family they are. My aunt Darlene told me a quote I'd heard many times before, but only then did I truly understand it. "You can pick your friends, but you can't pick your family." More need not be said.

∽∾∾

My heart skipped a beat on that afternoon of January 5 when I walked through the door of our home, and my wife, Sarah, told me that our son and his two children had been involved in an automobile accident and had been taken to a nearby hospital. A mental flashback blocked all immediate awareness as I recalled the moment years before when two policemen arrived at our door when we were living in Germany to tell us that Steven, who was then thirteen years of age, had been struck by a truck and was in the hospital. He had been on his way into Bad Godesberg, a suburb of Bonn where we lived, to procure a ski pass photograph since he and his mother were leaving the next day on a ski trip to Switzerland. They never made the trip. Steven was hospitalized for almost six months, and he endured numerous operations and a leg amputation.

Suddenly my mind returned to the present, and I anxiously telephoned the emergency room of the hospital to inquire about the condition of our son and his children. The reply was, "They are here, but there are no life-threatening injuries." Somewhat relieved, I departed for the hospital.

My sense of relief was short-lived. When I arrived at the

hospital, I was ushered into a waiting room with one chair, a sofa, and bare walls—a very unfriendly space. A highway patrolman entered carrying a clipboard of reports and bearing a blank countenance. He said, "Sir, you know there has been an automobile accident. Your son did not survive the crash. He was killed instantly on impact from a vehicle that struck him directly on the driver's side." Declared dead at the scene of the accident, he had not been brought to the hospital. Only the children, who had incurred minor injuries, were there. I was speechless, and a deathly silence filled the room as if no sound would ever be heard again.

The emptiness of the moment was indescribable. It was very different from the empty helplessness I had often experienced at Steven's bedside in the intensive care unit of the German hospital. There was a finality about this emptiness. By his bed I could at least hold his hand, bathe his forehead with a cool, damp cloth when his temperature soared, offer a comforting word, or kiss him good-bye until the next visit. All of that was replaced by a final emptiness, a vacuum. He was gone, taken from us in a moment. In the days and months that followed, however, I would discover time and again that Steven was still with us in his poetry, through which I could sense the beat of his heart.

From his childhood Steven was delightfully and keenly sensitive to the world around him. He seemed to have been born with a twinkle in his eye and an insatiable, patient curiosity for all things. When he was working with mechanical toys or objects that had been taken apart, little could deter him until he had solved the mystery of how all of the pieces fit back together.

Perhaps his unique modes of expression were a foreshadowing of his linguistic gifts, which would later flourish in English, German, Italian, and Native American languages. Once as our four young sons sat at the dinner table, perhaps wearied from an afternoon at the beach, the food was turned into projectiles not only directed at their mouths but at one another. As the activity peaked, my wife's hand forcefully came down on the table as she said, "Steven, people do not eat like that."

He (only four years of age) replied, "Mommy, we're not people. We're children."

∽∾∽

I do not know quite where to begin. When Steven died, the children moved in with their mother, who lived about ten miles away from the Cedar Grove house. She and Steven were divorced. When I first opened the door to the old farmhouse, evidence of him was everywhere. It was difficult to take. An old manual wheelchair sat solemnly empty on the front porch where he had hoped to repair it. In the kitchen window hung the stained glass city seal of Bonn, Germany, his mother and I had once given to him. High above the kitchen stove in the corner of a shelf rested a clay totem image he had made as a boy. On the landing leading to the large family room in the back of the house stood a breakfront filled with childhood memorabilia—his birth bracelet, his first tiny cowboy boots in which he had strutted about so proudly, and hand puppets—a

Steven skiing in the 1979
National Handicap Olympics

squirrel, a bird, and a tiger—he had so delighted to play and create funny conversations and stories. Atop the breakfront lying flat and difficult to see was the metal belt buckle embossed with the word *Love*, which he had been wearing when he had been hit by the truck. Next to it were a ski boot and outriggers, which are small fourteen- to sixteen-inch skis that fit on the end of the special poles made for leg-amputee skiers. Steven had learned to ski again after he had lost his leg, and in 1979, he won a gold medal in the competition then known as the National Handicap Olympics.[1] The medal lay there as well.

In a corner of the room his computer, as if frozen in time, was silently awaiting the touch of his hands. Books were everywhere—how he loved them—and of course, one could hardly find a space that was without evidence of the artwork, poetry, writings, and photographs of the children. They had become the focus and passion of his life!

Little was organized, except in the kitchen, where he spent numerous hours as a gourmet cook. Above the sink was a magnetic strip that held his extensive array of knives in place, as if suspended in time. Most things were within arms' reach. In recent years he had become increasingly dependent on a motorized wheelchair, and the general disorganization was evidence that he no longer could manage things as easily as he once had.

I walked into Dakotah's room, from which a spiral staircase led to the upstairs room Steven had added to the house. In the corner of the stairwell propped against the wall was the last leg prosthesis he had tried to use. Once more, time stood still for me. I could think of nothing but our lives in Germany before and after Steven's accident, which had left him with the loss of a limb.

∽∾∾

All of our sons entered a German school, Nicholas Cusanus Gymasium, except for David, the eldest, who came to Germany for a few months and attended a Goethe Institute to study German. He soon returned to the United States, however, to enter Drew University. The German school was quite unique, for it had special *Ausländerklassen*—that is, special classes for foreigners.

---

1   Today this competition is called Paralympics.

Centered in Bad Godesberg were many of the embassies from numerous nations since Bonn was the capital of Germany at that time. Timothy, Steven, and Mark progressed rapidly in their knowledge of German, and within six months they moved into regular classes with German students and were doing extremely well.

After a few years in a German school, Timothy, the next-to-the-eldest son, began to express an interest in attending a college or university in the United States. While his oral English skills were excellent, his English writing skills had suffered during the school years he was writing primarily in German. Hence, it was decided that for the eleventh and twelfth grades he would transfer to the American high school in Bad Godesberg, which was located just a few blocks from our apartment. His brothers, Steven and Mark, would follow suit a couple of years later.

Steven, though physically challenged through the loss of a leg, was as active as a beehive. Though only thirteen, he had already shown incredible gifts as an athlete before he lost his leg, and his interest in athletics continued. On fall weekends one found him announcing the play-by-play action of the American high school football games. His writing abilities blossomed as he began writing poetry, and his graphic art skills emerged in a surprisingly rapid manner. He excelled in his schoolwork, began playing the guitar in a band with his brothers, and grew spiritually as an active participant in the programs and worship of the American Protestant Church, where he was confirmed.

During his years at the American school, Steven began to develop an interest in Native American peoples and studies and entered a pilgrimage of reading that I followed closely. Desiring not only to know more of their history and culture, he yearned to understand the plight of these people. Such books as *God is Red, I Left My Heart at Wounded Knee,* and *Chronicles of Native American Protest* were carefully read and digested by him. His love of nature, so obvious from his childhood, was heightened by this literature, and all the more through numerous ski trips to the Swiss Alps and our summer camping trips to Italy, which took us through breathtaking mountain passes, by tranquil and raging streams, and into the silence of forests.

All of these experiences were shaping the whole and mature person he was becoming. Though taken from us, he left treasures of these early years in his poetry and artwork. I am not certain exactly when he began writing poetry; however, it was during his years in Germany, and he continued writing until the time of his death, spanning some thirty-five years.

ᑫᢍᡆ

Once again, I stared at the idle prosthesis beneath the staircase leaning gingerly against the wall as if poised in position for Steven to put it on. His own words about the accident came vividly to mind.

Still Alive and Well
or *A Funny Thing Happened on the Way across a Street or Promises, Promises or Where Were You when the Lights Went Out?* Or *Everything You Wanted to Know about Pain but Were Afraid to Ask*

Oh yes, he saw the yellow lights;
    With piercing truth they neared.
He'd heard of schizophrenic frights—
    Of these his mind he cleared.

In blood he lay, wet pools of red,
    So helplessly in shock.
He thought of silken-covered beds
    When finally came the doc.

"Will I go skiing tomorrow?"
What a stupid question—
Now's the time for pain and sorrow,
For medicine injection.

Come sirens, needles, one and all,
You puffed-up, boasting foe,
You think that I intend to fall?
Then pack, my friend, and go.

"Yes, Doc, my hope, what can I do?
You've told them I would die.
How I hate to disappoint you,
But, tell me, why should I?"

For two months after his accident Steven lay in the intensive care unit of the *Evangelisches Krankenhaus* (a Lutheran hospital in Bad Godesberg), sometimes called the *Wald Krankenhaus* (Forest Hospital) since it was located near a large forest. This was an extremely difficult time. Often he was at the brink of death, suffering from extremely high temperatures that might have caused brain damage had it not been for the watchful care of the nurses who packed him with ice when necessary. For thirty-nine days in succession he was taken to the operating room for diverse procedures, and his body diminished by some forty pounds. To suffer with your child as a parent is torture, but I could not possibly have seen things through his eyes, except as he described his experience in the following poems.

The IV

I've been lying here
forever;
The IV is getting thicker quicker.
I don't know

what happened then,
but I know what's happening
now.
The drops keep dripping—
drip,
drip,
drip.
My head is getting
lighter;
the sheets are getting
whiter.

Someone's been lying around here—
forget it.
It's time to clip the IV
in privy.
You're not trying to
heal me;
you're trying to
kill me.
The drips keep dropping—
drop,
drop,
drop.
My patience's growing
thinner.
Watch out!
Your patient's still a
winner.

Your patient's growing
thinner.
Watch out!
My patience's still a
winner.

Breakfast in Bed

Every single morning,
I get
breakfast in bed.

Rise and shine.
My eyes open
to whiteness:
the sheets,
the walls,
ceiling,
the nurses,
their dresses,
smiles.

Bon appétit.
My mouth opens to whiteness:
cream of wheat,
whites of eggs,
milk,
yogurt,
and pills—
little white ones.

This is how it goes—
day in,
day out—
service with a
Plaster-of-Paris smile
in a
Master-of-Paris style.

And
every single morning,

I get
breakfast in bed.

I don't like it.

After two months he was strong enough to be moved to a private room. High on the fifth floor of the hospital, he could look out over the beautiful, adjacent forest filled with regal pine and oak trees and occasionally see the soaring birds that often danced in the top branches. Steven mused,

Healing

Trapped,
imprisoned
by no fault
of my own
between the sheets.
I watch
the eagles
circle slowly.

As I passed through the doorway and returned to the kitchen, the sun beamed through the stained glass seal of the city of Bonn hanging in the window, casting an elegant multi-rayed reflection on my beige-colored jacket.

Steven at Trafalgar Square, London

Instantly mental visions of our lives in Europe flashed across my memory like lightning. Living outside the United States had a lasting impact on Steven linguistically, intellectually, and socially. He developed skills in German and English rather quickly. In the summers it seemed quite natural for him to work as a translator at international camps in Switzerland and Austria with youth his own age or older. Our annual Thanksgiving trips to London by train from Bonn to Ostende, Belgium, and from there via hovercraft or ferry to Dover, England, expanded his vision of himself, others, and the world, and the enchantment of a summer trip to Paris effervesced from his picturesque imagination.

Arch of Triumph, Parisian Yearning

Arch of triumph, Parisian yearning, arching now,
 for sure triumphant;
long nights of lonely aloneness, now in this,
 conquered for the moment;

Drunk with self, in need of other self,
 now willing, as nature, to exploit,
 more wanting, as nature, to explore;
 end endless night! End endless dreams!
Full of plotting, full of acquisition,
 full of need, full of desire;

And ending now, at least for the now,
 left prepared and adorned for battle,
 or at least for a tangle;
surely a tangle sufficient to sober the self,
 to leave me yet drunk with other self
 and to make drunk the other self, with love
 and love's juices;
ah, but still only sufficient till the tangling

is over;

Arch of triumph, Parisian yearning, arching now,
　　for sure triumphant;
long nights of lonely aloneness, now in this,
　　conquered for the moment;

now this Parisian yearning, rested but restless, ready;
now this Parisian yearning, dream-drunk, prepared
　　coming;

I see in you surely more than Napoleon
　　might—crazed building, or was it
　　Napoleon might—crazed building
　　who saw more, and now in these
　　times is providing?

Arch of triumph, in the morning,
　　morning sun exploring anachronistic archways
　　and huge stones: Do me justice! Which is no
　　justice. Proclaim me victor! Which is no victory.
　　Satisfy! What deeper desire in me now itself
　　queries that is no deeper desire but merely
　　the life forces themselves searching;
And arch of triumph, in the noontide,
　　bathed in beauty, beauties with bathing suits
　　or without, preferably without, their arches
　　too in a sun stupor, the brightness worshipping.
　　Do me justice!

And arch of triumph, in the evening,
　　painted now love, in tender evening colors,
　　saying, "I am in these love colors attired,
　　readily awaiting an augmentation by your

love colors." Do me justice!

And this is it now; in Parisian night heat
　　with other self my way arching, I finally
　　too am arching!
And it is so much simpler than I would make;
　　behold and witness these many arches,
　　some this color, some that color, some this size,
　　some that size, and since the beginning
　　of time, each arching, each loving!
Now I am arching and loving each—especially
　　in Parisian night heat this one!
Praise be to God in heaven for this one!
And praise be to Satan in hell for this one!
And praise be to you, and praise be to me
　　for this one;

Arch of triumph, Parisian yearning, arching now,
　　for sure triumphant;
long nights of lonely aloneness, now in this,
　　conquered for the moment!

His affection for the city of Bonn, where he spent his teenage
years, was cleverly expressed in German.

Ich wäre lieber in Bonn[2]

1.　Ich bin durch die ganze Welt gereist,
　　　　von Schweden bis Amerika;
　　und die verschied'nsten Essen gespeist,
　　　　Spaghetti und Tapioka.

　　Nun lieg' ich hier mit Sandwich im Mund,

2　English: I would rather be in Bonn.

unter der schön' Hawaii Sonn',
und denke zurück, das ist der Grund—
ich wäre lieber in Bonn!

Refrain:
Ich wäre lieber in Bonn, am romantischen Rhein,
ich wäre lieber in Bonn, da schmeckt der billigste Wein;
ich vermisse die Uni, Museen, Helmut & Co.;
ich träum' von Oper, Theater, Bonner Sommer Show;
da werde ich begrüßt
mit einem Bonner Kuß;
ich wäre lieber in Bonn.

2. Ich bin bis zum Nordpol gefahren,
    hab' geangelt mit Eskimos;
Senoritas, hab' ich erfahren,
    mögen nicht nur Caballeros.
Ich sitze im Pariser Lokal,
    und flirt' mit einer Prima Donn'.
In Rom schau ich ein Endpokal
    aber ich wäre lieber in Bonn!

3. Die schönsten Städte wie Wien und Rom
    sind mir durch Reisen wohl bekannt—
Kairo, Oslo, Neu Dehli, und Qom;
    hab' ich damit ein Paar genannt.
Nun bin ich im Palast Buckingham,
    so traumhaft schön die Stadt London!
Ich sag' der Queen, "Your Highness, Mam,"
    "Ich wäre lieber in Bonn."

Saddened, I sat down for a few minutes. Yet an inner peace
came over me like the stillness of ocean waters at low tide when
there is no wind. I'm not sure how much time passed. As if

coming out of a trance, my eyes fell on the desk behind me where a notebook teetered on the edge at a precarious angle. I thought it might be one of the children's in which he or she had prepared schoolwork. I could not be sure, however, for it seemed Steven had notebooks everywhere. He was a list maker, a recorder of daily events and family life, and he wrote poetry on every imaginable type and size of paper. I had to be careful not to throw anything away, for a poem could be written on the back of a used envelope.

When I opened the notebook, it was filled with poems in his own hand. The first one I came upon was titled "Lorelei." Immediately, as if someone had inserted a DVD into my brain, I could see Steven traveling on the Rhine River, which flowed through Bonn. He was fascinated by this river, which bustled with commercial boat and barge traffic. It was lined with elegant castles and enchanting castle ruins harboring secrets and stories of a rich European past to be discovered and retold. The legendary and magical stories of the Rhine often present in literature, opera, and folk songs intrigued him. The famous Lorelei rock on the Rhine near St. Goarshausen inspired many tales and legends.

Lorelei

Goddess willing, the creeks will rise.
She'll wash her body and baptize
saints and sinners one and the same—
nothing sacred, profane by name.

Though all are chosen, few survive.
Dolphin, please show me how to dive.
Whale, will you teach me how to sing?
Flying fish, lend me a sleek new wing.

Lorelei sings a melody;
she lives supernaturally,
her magic—harmony of song,
and all of us can sing along.

I went outside for a breath of fresh air, paused, and looked around the property surrounding the house. On the right side of it were two large sheds Steven had placed there for his children's pleasure. They called them their chalets. Over the last four years they had become storage sheds since lightning had destroyed a small building behind the farmhouse that overflowed with numerous boxes of books whose contents had been transferred to the chalets. I went back to the shed, where I had placed the large footlocker from the old Cadillac, and opened it again.

In between a plethora of folders I found a neatly wrapped envelope marked "Save." I opened it very carefully so as not to damage the contents. Tears filled my eyes as I found the picture of a clown (ca. six inches by nine inches) I had given to him at the world premiere performance of the opera *Pentheus* by Italian composer Francesco Valdambrini. I was cast in the leading role of the Greek god Dionysus and Steven as my alter ego or companion Pseudo-Dionysus. This occurred during my second year as a leading baritone of the Bonn Opera Company (*Theater der Stadt Bonn*). The stage director, Virginio Puecher, had auditioned numerous young boys from the surrounding area for the role but could find no one satisfactory. Pseudo-Dionysus would have to dance well and play the tambourine. In other words, he had to have a superb sense of rhythm and elegant poise. At a rehearsal one afternoon, in frustration Puecher asked me if one of my sons might try out for the part. Steven was delighted to do so and was immediately cast in the role. He performed magnificently, and one critic described him as a mini Marcel Marceau, the famous French mime. The performances of the opera were in the spring, a number of months before Steven's accident.

I marveled at his acting gifts, the fluidity of his movements, and his uncanny ability to grasp the difficult rhythms that shifted swiftly from one time signature to another four or five times within sixteen to twenty-four bars of music. Once he had mastered these passages, he never faltered in performance.

∽∾∾

Steven realized clearly that he was an American youth growing up in Germany. While for many transplanted young people such transitions were extremely difficult, his linguistic gifts made his cultural and social integration much easier than it was for those who spoke only English. Even when he returned to school after his accident, he was extremely enthusiastic about the possibility of continuing the study of Italian. His travels, language skills, and reading about other cultures, such as those of Native Americans, shaped a broad *Weltanschauung* (worldview) of life and humankind. One of his teenage poems poignantly expresses his maturing vision of himself and others.

My Family

Black is my brother,
Puerto Rican is my sister,
Liberty is my mother,
And God is my father,
My family—peace,
Our world—love.
Forever God shall reign on high,
In unison my sister,
In unison my brother,
My family in peace.

The German school, Nicholas Cusanus Gymnasium, that Steven attended was filled with youth from all over the world whose parents were affiliated with various embassies in Bonn. His first class included students from fifteen nations. Two of his best friends were a brother and a sister from Venezuela, and the drummer in the band in which he played with his brothers was an African American. He was living his emerging worldview.

Two of his early poems express the pain he felt for oppressed peoples, Native Americans in both instances.

Talking Leaves

Talking leaves
meant pilgrims' progress
talking leaves
made pilgrims' promises
talking leaves
rallied reception
talking leaves
hid deception
talking leaves
ordered relocation
talking leaves
guaranteed distinction
talking leaves
almost spelled extinction
talking leaves
you're wondering
whether
what was said
is true

Strong Wind

Like a strong wind in the face;
my people saw them come.

Like a strong wind in the face;
   my people tried to understand.

Like a strong wind in the face;
   my people sickened.

Like a strong wind in the face;
   my people died—
Like a strong wind in the face.

His worldview, however, began from within the family. His three brothers had played a vital part in his recovery in the hospital. When he was in the intensive care unit, the family members could visit him only fifteen minutes a day. Steven's accident had occurred just ten days before Christmas. The eldest brother, David, had returned from the United States for the holidays and accompanied his other brothers, Sarah, and me to visit Steven in the hospital. We shared the time, a few minutes two by two at his bedside. Tears flowed as I saw his brothers at every visit hold his outstretched hands on each side of the bed.

One need only read what he wrote about this mother to understand that his worldview began with family.

On Knowing and Growing

I know my mother knows
something about me
I'll never know
and my mother knows I know
something about her
she will never know
and we are both content to know
what we will never know—
but is there one among us
content to know

and never grow
for you can grow
and not know
but you cannot know
and not grow

Steven's brush with death in his youth enriched him with a maturity that it is difficult to describe. He was never content to know and not grow. I think this is something he had learned from his very wise mother. It would have been difficult for him to see beyond boundaries without this vision.

In the footlocker I found a journal he had kept sporadically. In thumbing through it I came upon this passage about his mother recorded on October 22, 1980:

> Sarah had her 50th birthday just a few days ago. It's hard to imagine what a time of contemplation and reflection this must have been for her. She is such a strong woman and a very beautiful one too. She has sent me a breath-taking shot of her made many years ago, and I'm not sure whether there has ever been a woman more beautiful. Her beauty is deep though, beauty that comes from the spirit. She loves selflessly and she loves tragically, if need be. She's forever concerned. Here are some words for her on her 50th.

Rabbits

I remember
lying flat
unable to move
but you looked out of the window
for me
and you told me
how the rabbits

were coming out of the bushes
to stand
to eat
to converse
to play
all in the moonlight

I'll never forget
the rabbits

Next to the diary was a very large envelope marked "Save." Upon examination I discovered that it included his piano-vocal books for voice study at Duke University: *Vaccai Vocalises, Early American Songs* arranged by Aaron Copland, songs by Brahms, Mozart, and others. Packed neatly beside the large envelope was his undergraduate diploma from Duke University inscribed with *magna cum laude.* I dropped to the floor of the shed and reminisced.

Steven's brother Timothy, who was almost two years his elder, had entered Duke University upon completion of his studies at the Bonn American High School. Steven and his younger brother Mark had also spent at least two years at the same school to improve their English skills hoping to enter an American university. Both would follow Timothy and matriculate at Duke University. All three brothers had double majors, in Steven's case German and art design. He honed his creative writing skills in English courses as well.

Music continued to play a vital role in his life. As a child, as did brothers Timothy and Mark, Steven had studied piano when we lived in Princeton, New Jersey. In Bonn he also learned French horn and played bass guitar in a band with his brothers. He had an excellent ear for music and enjoyed singing as well. Hence, it was not surprising that he began studying voice with my former voice teacher, Professor John Hanks, in the Duke University music department.

At Duke Timothy once again organized a musical group known as *One Real Band*. His instrument was piano or keyboard, and when Steven arrived at the university, he began playing bass guitar for the group. Mark became a percussionist in the band when he, too, entered Duke.

During the Duke years Steven wrote a plethora of lyrics for some of the band's songs, many of which were set to music by Timothy. The centrality and importance of music in Steven's life was unquestionable.

I Want to Feel the Music

I want to feel the music
    right down into my toes.
I want to feel the music
    that everybody knows.
For if you feel the music
    then you will love and share,
and you can dance for ever,
    for ever in the air.

I want to feel the music
    down to my finger tips
I want to feel the music
    upon my lover's lips
telling me, "Feel the music,
    just feel it everywhere,
so we can dance together,
    together in the air."

Music opens eyes to see
    what's not been seen before.
It fills you with surprises
    and keeps you wanting more.
You'll wonder why there's hatred,

till hatred's up and gone;
the miracle's the music
    you'll feel it coming on.

Music can make you giving,
    more than you have to give.
Music opens ears to hear
    the sounds that help you live.
It can take a monotone
    and change it to a song;
so when you hear the music,
    why don't you sing along!

"Aegyptophithecus" as drawn by Steven Forris Kimbrough

Steven's graphic art skills continued to develop at the university, particularly in the charcoal and pencil mediums. His talent was unequivocally evident in a commission he received from a leading anthropologist named Dr. Elwyn Simons of Duke University to make a drawing of *Aegyptophithecus*, an ancestor of man and ape. The drawing appeared in the *New York Times* (February 7, 1980), *Newsweek* (February 18, 1980), and *Time*

(February 18, 1980), and it has since been used in a number of books on anthropology.

I put the Duke diploma back in its secure place, the envelope marked "Save." As I did so, I noticed at the end of the row of file folders and envelopes there was a large, square, flat package carefully wrapped, sealed, and postmarked to Steven in 1980. I hesitated to open it, as he had addressed it to himself. It was a sacrosanct matter in our family that you do not open someone else's mail. Then of course it dawned on me that now it was my responsibility to open it since he was no longer alive. The old paper tape, dry and crinkled from so many years of storage, popped open easily as my knife blade slid through it. As a shrink-wrapped white edge emerged, I knew immediately what I had in my hands. It was the last LP recorded by *One Real Band,* on which he played bass guitar. They had played together for the last time at the dinner after Steven's first wedding. With utmost care I took the edge of the LP cover between my thumb and fingers and pulled it from its secure hiding place of thirty years. I remembered well the photograph of the band members inside the cover but had forgotten what songs they had recorded. When I turned over the cover to read the titles, my eyes fell first on "Rita's Song."

Once more everything else was blanked from my mind, as if I were locked in a vault of silence and all the rest of the world did not exist.

It was during his university years that we were finally able to achieve a court judgment in Steven's favor. Five individuals had witnessed the accident in which he was injured, and all of them signed affidavits stating that Steven was in the right and that the driver of the truck that had struck him had run through a red light. It seems inconceivable, but it took eight years to litigate the case in Germany. By this time Steven was near completion of his studies at Duke University.

His deep concern and open heart for oppressed persons was

once again shown when he asked me to assist him with providing some matching funds for the bail bond fund of the National Council of Churches in New York City. He had learned of an excessive bail set for a Native American woman named Rita in Oklahoma, who, as a poor, single mother, could not meet the high bail set by the court. She had no option whatsoever to care for her young child while she was incarcerated. If funds could be raised locally for half of the required bail, the bail bond fund would match those funds to enable her to make bail prior to trial. By securing the money through treasury bills, Steven was able to provide ten thousand dollars of the required amount, which helped achieve the necessary goal. This selfless gesture, utilizing a portion of the funds from the court settlement, was evidence of his big heart and desire to reach out to others. Fortunately since the funds were secured in treasury notes, they were later returned to him via the bail bond fund.

Steven's deep feelings for Rita and her plight were set to music with lyrics he wrote for her, a song often performed by *One Real Band.*

Rita's Song (You Were There)

It took a hundred winters just to see
that the once mighty buffalo don't roam—
they're not roaming anymore.

It took two hundred winters just to see
that once the mighty eagle cannot fly home—
he won't fly home anymore.

You can't race the rivers running freely
they have courses you cannot run.
You can't move the mountains in a moment
against forces like the sun.

O Rita, before I heard your story
I know I knew;
O Rita, before I saw your face
well I saw you,
for you were there at Wounded Knee,
you were there at Alcatraz,
you prepared the first Thanksgiving feast,
and you were there from the very start,
and you are there right now in every heart,
and you'll be there till there's everlasting peace.
It's not very hard to see
this is what was meant to be—
instead of living apart
we're living part of eternity
and it feels so good to know
that there are others who can hear it—
the great silence flowing between us now
is the sound of the Great Spirit.

It took two hundred winters just to find
that once you listen to the trees
you learn to listen easily.
It took two hundred winters just to find
that you cannot fabricate the free—
something is free naturally.

You can't play with people or their ponies;
they have reason, reason all their own.
You can't torture nature, Mother Nature,
and her seasons (not yet fully grown).

O Rita, before I heard your story
I know I knew;
O Rita, before I saw your face
well I saw you,

for you were there at Wounded Knee,
you were there at Alcatraz,
you prepared the first Thanksgiving feast,
and you were there from the very start,
and you are there right now in every heart,
and you'll be there till there's everlasting peace.

Though the following poem did not appear on the LP, it reflects Steven's empathy and affection for Native American life, culture, and integration with nature:

The Song of the Morning
The Sun-God's Singing

With the sweetness of birth
Emerges from the perils of night
Come O Sun-God to sing
When the stench has passed—
To the blueness given in
Come O Sun-God to sing

Like the wetness of life the bleeding is done
The pain in the dark has vanished
The dew like the wetness of innocence wreaks
From the snows to the sea
So the life-cord is severed
Releasing the Sun-God
From Mother-Nature
As the Great Spirit plays with the moon
Tossing him to and fro
Into an abyss
While the stars run away white-eyed

Be the Sun-God unleashed he rises
To paint with colors the dawn

And he paints
His masterpiece
With the crack of his glare
The dew gave in
Make way dead-life for the Sun-God
The colors light so the red-people can see
In the morning

The red-women go up to wash
For they now have lights
The red-men cough up yesterday
For they now have lights
The bear moves to the river and the kingfisher dives
Fires pop and crack so the red-people can eat
For they now have lights
Buffalo graze on the plains with heads to the sky
The pintos shake their manes
For they now have lights

The colors light so the red-people can see
In the morning
When the lights have been broken
The loving all rest
And the lights of the Sun-God bring meaning
And the smell of meats take over
And wrestling boys begin
And fool-hearted braves grow anxious
And beautiful maidens dream
And elders plan
And babies cry

And rays streak the heavens
And geese make their formation
And the stream plays once more
To the tune of the chickadee

And all the people in the teepees are happy
For the promise of the Great Spirit
To send by the Sun-God
After each bleak dusk
The maiden of life to the red-people
Has been kept

Now they can start a new day
To the singing of the Sun-God
The maiden of life's awakening voice
The colors light so the red-people can see
In the morning
They like this song too
It has life

My gaze was transfixed on the album cover. I have no idea how long I sat there almost in a trance. After a while I picked up the postmarked cover with Steven's own handwriting. Why had he addressed the package to himself? Then I remembered. Of course, he had learned this practice in Germany, where a postmarked envelope mailed to yourself that includes something of your own creativity—poetry, prose, a drawing—is considered a valid confirmation of copyright.

❧

I had gotten quite cold, for it was the heart of winter in North Carolina, and I had been sitting on the floor of an unheated, outdoor shed. I got up and decided to return to the house. I put my hands between the file folders to make space for the packaged LP. The folder to the left bore the designation "McDade Road Property." I could not resist pulling it out and opening it. Inside was a surveyor's plot of the property Steven first purchased in Cedar Grove. It was impossible to escape the flood tide of reminiscences that overwhelmed me.

Not long after his graduation from Duke University, Steven purchased approximately ten acres of land with two dwellings on the property in the rural community of Cedar Grove, North Carolina. He was thrilled to be living in the woods perfumed by the smell of trees, grass, and plants and teeming with all sorts of intriguing living creatures. Part of the headwaters of the Eno River were on the property, and the building of a dam by a family of beavers just below these waters and by the roadside was an annual occurrence that was exciting to observe.

To be able to plant a garden all his own for the first time since he was a child was a special delight. We had lived in Hillsborough, North Carolina, when I was a graduate student at Duke University. In the back of our house was about a half of an acre of land that we had plowed so we could plant a large garden. Though Steven was a very young boy, he was old enough to drop some seeds into a furrow, cover them with soil, and watch them grow. Now as a grown man, he could revive those memories in planting his own garden.

Within months of graduation and the purchase of the Cedar Grove property, Steven married. He longed to love a partner and to be loved by her.

I Am a Love-man

I am a love-man
and I invite you
to be my love-woman
for there is nothing
more simple
and more beautiful
than this
save perhaps that which is both
love-man and love-woman
love-child

Unfortunately after a few years the marriage ended in divorce. Still he longed for love and family. His disappointment in love was extremely painful.

Love Was a Four-letter Word

The first one
came
shortly thereafter
well-perfumed
and full of adjectives
the words
picked me up
and the scent
swept me away
I remember this letter
so very well
because I remembered you
so very well
that
was the first one

The second one
came
after a while
perfumed
and full of words
the adjectives
picked me up
but the scent
what was it again
I remember this letter
so well
because
I remembered you

so well
that
was the second one

The third one
came
sometime
stale fragrance
and full of not much
it picked away
and I sensed
what was happening
I remember this letter
well
because
you had forgotten me
O well
that was the third one

The fourth one
came
finally
colorless
and full of adjectives again
I picked it up
then I
threw it away
sensible
I forgot this letter
and you
all together

Love was a four-letter word

Fortunately he continued to write and to produce exquisite charcoal drawings. What he could not find in a loving relationship, to some extent he found in caressing words or a piece of charcoal.

The burning desire to love and to be loved by someone overpowered him, and he married again. More than anything else he wanted to establish a happy home with children, and from this marriage two were born, a son named Dakotah and a daughter named Savannah. How he loved them and their mother passionately. Of this marriage he wrote,

Always Home

I am always home
whenever
I lay eyes on you
heaven let me in
the day we met

And when
I lose my way
I close my eyes
and see that I'm
as close to heaven
as I'll get

Tragically for Steven this marriage also ended in divorce. The years leading up to the separation and ultimate divorce were torture for him. For a time he sought to drown his sorrow in alcohol, and now and then he had bouts with excessive drinking. Soon, however, he realized that he was going to be the primary caregiver or Mr. Mom, as he put it, for his children. The house that he and his second wife had purchased at the time of their marriage, which was also located in the community of Cedar

Grove (almost three acres of land with a beautiful pond and an old farmhouse), continued to be the primary residence for him and the children after his second wife had moved away. Realizing his responsibility to care for the children, he managed to overcome the alcohol problem.

I remember well a tearful phone call from him at this trying time when he said, "Dad, all I have ever wanted was a happy family. At least I have two wonderful children." The sadness of the failure in love broke his heart, and he wrote,

Under the Bridge

Every rose that I ever picked
    For you as you walked out the door
Floats petalless beneath the bridge
    The Bridge of Love that's nevermore.

And every card I ever wrote
    By hand not bought at any store
Is waterlogged and sinks beneath
    The Bridge of Love that's nevermore.

Every song that I ever wrote
    Countless—I never kept the score
Is aimlessly adrift beneath
    The Bridge of Love that's nevermore.

Steven was a persistent romantic longing for love of a mate that somehow seemed to elude him. The sense of affection expressed beneath mistletoe at Christmas awakened in him a vision of life as it should be.

Mistletoe

Refrain:
Take me back to Mistletoe
    take me back where I belong,
where the sweet spring water runs
    where I'm healthy and so strong.

Take me back to Mistletoe
    don't try to take me away,
if you do then rest assured
    that is where my heart will stay.

Mom and Daddy split apart,
    Mommy wanted to be free;
no one had the guts or love
    to first check it out with me.

Bounced back and forth—house to house
    like buffalo children roam,
but mistletoe's still my house,
    yes, mistletoe's still my home.

Refrain

The grass may be green, greener
    on the fence's other side,
but the pledge "till death we part"
    was not made to be decried.

I'll take grass in whatever,
    whatever color it be;
if you decide to leave it
    better check things out with me.

Refrain

Now I was desperately cold and had to return to the house. I closed the footlocker, placed the three volumes of *The Cadillac Poems* under my right arm, put the lock through the hasp on the shed door, closed it, and went back into the warmth of the house. Everywhere there was evidence of Dakotah and Savannah—photographs, poetry, drawings, etc. They had become the center of Steven's world, and their every achievement was his greatest joy. He marveled at their learning gifts and the quickness with which they grasped the simplest and most complex things, which was probably the motivation for a poem he wrote when they were eight and nine years of age.

One Big Garden

1. We come to Kindergarten
        and little do we know
    that school is one big garden
        where knowledge wants to grow.

2. First grade—we learn the basics
        to cipher, read, and write;
    like sun and earth and water
        we start to see the light.

    Refrain:
    My pencil is my hoe,
        my binder is my field;
    I study hard and knowledge is
        the harvest that I yield.
    My vision is my plow,
        my books are all the rows,
    and in pursuit of excellence
        one reaps just what one sows.

3. Second grade—seeds we've planted
        begin to move and sprout;
   our teacher is the gardener
        as we figure things out.

4. Third grade—all we are learning
        like roots is taking hold;
   our confidence is growing:
        we're smarter and we're bold.

Refrain

5. Fourth grade—we now are reaching,
        we're reaching for the sky,
   leaves and stems and branches,
        we'll reach them, if we try.

6. We came to Kindergarten
        and little did we know
   that school was one big garden
        where knowledge wants to grow.

Refrain

❦

I picked up one of the books of *The Cadillac Poems*, sat down at
Steven's desk, which was his maternal grandmother's old treadle
Singer sewing machine, and began to read. The first poem was
curiously titled "The Man and the Frog."

The Frog—he jumps
to get somewhere
the Man—he jumps
to conclusions

The Frog—he seems
to get somewhere
the Man—he seems
to get confusion

Another poem described little creatures that regularly leave their silk-spun traces throughout the old farmhouse and its surroundings.

The Spider

Spider spin on
weave a web
for here and now
span the ages
build the bridges
so the dew
in dew time
may hang once again
in morning splendor

I could not resist and read on and on. With every lyric I felt the beating of Steven's heart in the rhythm of the words and the lilting of phrases.

ODES TO NATURE

Painted Pony

1. I need some new shoes
   my mane is a mess
   with so many miles to go

   But I still have the power
   and the pedigree
   to make it to one final show

   I've long lost my rider
   my back is now bare
   I'm naked and that sure feels good
   sure feels good

2. Let me chase one more buffalo
   jump one more fence
   rear up and paw at the sky

   Let me gallop and cantor
   and run with the wind
   this is a good day to die

   Let me taste the sweet water
   for one last time
   and I will be ready to go
   ready to go

3. Now I'm cleaned up and painted
   looking real fine
   for a date that I'm not gonna miss

   I'm red and I'm yellow
   I'm black and I'm white
   and this is the apocalypse

(It will be) quick but not painless
then over and out
and we'll start all over again
over again

All the Time

There is a dog
that roams the streets
at night
and sometimes during the day

Chewing milk cartons
from trash cans
and she barks now and then too

Some say she is rabid

And no one will look at her or after her

She smells

This dog
is dripping milk
tomorrow there will be
puppies

There is a dog
that roams the streets
at night
and sometimes
during the day

Once a Blossom

Once a blossom
now honey
once a meadow
mother's milk
and all the tears
that fall
were once
a mighty ocean
once mulberry
now silk

Once a feeling
now expression
once a body
now a soul
and every diamond
once upon a time
began as coal

Bolder than Boulder?

I have heard the sea lion
yelping helplessly
on the shoreline
amongst oil-slippery boulders

As the morning sun breaks
there is yelping
impatient pups
are hungry for more
than sickly seafood

As the noonday sun beats down
there is yelping
bewildered parents
can't believe
their pups are boots

As the evening sun smolders
there is yelping
a still-proud pack gathers
to recall
the good old games

Amongst oil-slippery boulders
on the shoreline
yelping helplessly
I have heard the sea lion

I have heard the sea
roaring restlessly
against the shore
making boulders oil-slippery

As the morning sun breaks
there is roaring
an embarrassed sea
is ashamed
to lap ashore

As the noon-day sun beats down
there is roaring
a riderless wave
misses
the back-scratching cowboys

As the evening sun smolders
there is roaring
the moon's romantic reflector
recalls young lovers
in one foot of water.

Making boulders oil-slippery
roaring restlessly
against the shore
I have heard the sea

I have seen the lion
yawning lazily
and occasionally snoring
atop pre-fab boulders

As the morning sun breaks
there is yawning
a curious kitten
wonders what Daddy
does for a living

As the noonday sun beats down
there is yawning
a fly-covered rib eye
fails to satisfy
any feline fantasies

As the evening sun smolders
there is yawning
a kingdomless king
recalls a reign
on the plain

Atop prefab boulders
yawning lazily
and occasionally snoring
I have seen the lion

I have heard and seen men lying
conquering without regard
leaving nothing unshorn
acting bolder than the boulders themselves

As the morning sun breaks
there is conquering
I can break the water
I can harbor the sea

As the noonday sun beats down
there is conquering
I can break the beast
I can tame the wild

As the evening sun smolders
there is conquering
I can break the breeze
I can harness the wind

Acting bolder than the boulders themselves
leaving nothing unshorn
conquering without regard
I have heard and seen men lying

In the Dead of Winter

1. In the dead of winter
   it must have been spring

   The birds began singing
   the flowers began blooming
   the snows began melting
   the rivers began rising

2. In the dead of winter
   it must have been spring

   I couldn't help singing
   as you began blooming
   we couldn't help melting
   as our passions began rising

   In the dead of winter
   I'm sure
   it must have been spring

Quilt of Many Colors

Is there anything as beautiful
as Autumn?
Is there anything as beautiful as Fall?—
leaves me breathless and blinded
by a quilt of many colors.
Is there anything as beautiful as Fall

Is there anything as beautiful
as Winter
waiting for the first snowflake to fall
all cozy and quiet

in my quilt of many colors
waiting for the first snowflake to fall?

Is there anything as beautiful
as Springtime?
Some insist it is the prettiest of all
shrouded from the showers
by my quilt of many colors.
Some insist it is the prettiest of all

Is there anything as beautiful
as Summer?
Ah but Summer's just an angel 'bout to fall
into the arms of autumn
into the quilt of many colors.
Is there anything as beautiful as fall?

The Fall

Feel the fall
so colorful
earth tones
dressing ancient earth bones

Fall in love
love in fall
autumn feelings
freely falling

Feel the fall
breathe air
swell the breeze
so crisp so clear

Feel the fall
see the sun
so bright so clear
colors amaze season ablaze

Feel the fall
hear the leaves
as they're falling
loud and clear

Feel the fall
taste the fruits
now touch the earth
she is so near

Feel the fall
so wonderful
so wondrous
evening dawns

Darkness falls
all alone
I in fall
fall in me

First Flower of the Spring

First flower of the spring
You make me want to sing
And though you're blossoming for all
I'm feeling finally
That it is just for me
So very naturally after all

You see the world
In a different way
Opening yourself each day
And all you really want to do is be
Reaching for the sun
Reaching for someone
Who wants to see
And wants to be
With you (first flower)
Loving every hour
Love will bring
I just want to sing
I feel it happening
First flower of the spring

Première fleur du printemps
Tu me fait chanter
Et bien que tu fleurisses pour tous
Il me semble que c'est pour moi seul
Tellement naturelle et après tout

Moon Song

I see the moon tonight
but what does she see
as she waits patiently
each passing
to bare herself fully
to reveal her secrets
to share her soul
as only a sister can share

Blue Sister the Moon
there are those beneath the haze
who still feel your powerful reflection
who still praise your each new passing
who still pray in your shining silence
who forever your way gaze
into the cold night air

She has no fear
she fears no evil
for evil is only a word
She has no fear
for we are still here
and here is more than a word

Our prayer is but a breath
but a breath is all we are
Oh Blue Sister the Moon
the man that you once knew
has travelled far
and will be returning
very soon

Amazing Sky

Polaris is pirouetting tonight
And even in the daytime she is bright
Just close your eyes and orient
Yourself and you will see
She is always up there
Shining down on you and me
Amazing Sky

Big Dipper is revolving keeping time
Every day she comes around
And then she climbs
She fills herself with stardust
And pours it on us all
She scoops us up and drops us
Just to watch us fall
Through this Amazing Sky

And whenever anybody ever wonders
How it is I love you
Don't ever wonder what to say
When you reply
I love you like a
Falling star
Loves a darkening sky

Constellations like a halo
Like a crown
With their stations their revelations
Merry go round
Just hitch a ride
Up on that horse
And watch to feel the sting
Of one star-clad scorpion

Now the Midnight Sun Is Setting

1. They used to lumber
   polar bear
   over the ice
   and through the whiteness

   Royally garbed
   in frosted fur
   sporting icicle beards
   searching for game
   searching for games
   the lumbering life
   is all work
   and all play

   Rearing proudly
   pawing skyward
   steaming breath
   full of life

   Rearing cubs
   drawing close to
   steaming breast
   so full of life

   But strange scents
   spelled danger
   and where they were sent
   smelled even stranger

   They used to lumber
   polar bear
   but now the midnight sun is setting

2. They used to slumber
   polar bear
   inside their igloos
   loving through the night

   Royally garbed
   in frosted fur
   sporting icicle beards
   searching for game
   searching for games
   the lumbering life
   is all work
   and all play

   Cheering loudly
   gnawing on fresh seal
   steaming breath
   full of life

   Rearing children
   drawing close to
   steaming breast
   so full of life

   But strange sense came
   and overtook them
   dollars and cents came
   and forsook them

   They used to slumber
   polar bear
   but now the midnight sun is setting

Prayer for the Sea Otter

1. Agile little otter
   playing like shellfish
   amidst the kelp
   not a care in the world
   abalone on the half shell
   bathing in the moonlight
   playing Marco Polo
   till three

   Skinny-dipping forever
   underwater acrobat
   the sea's your trapeze
   the current's your net
   making love
   on the crest of a wave
   agile little otter
   playing like shellfish

   Agile little otter
   more human than my best friend
   I pray for you tonight

2. Because
   the agile little otter
   is hunted selfishly
   amidst the yelps
   who cares about this world
   just abalone—the whole shell
   bathing is for bathtubs
   who in the world
   is Marco Polo

Skinny-dipping's for weirdos
give me a baseball bat
the sea's full of these
water-rats
Making money
on the crest of a grave
agile little otter hunted selfishly

Agile little otter
more human than my best friend
you are prey tonight

She cries

Little cubs suckle
droplets rolling from
their faces
such little things
much too young to see
what's there

She cries

Because she doesn't
know
what she will tell
them
when they are older

How do you say
your father is a coat

She cries

Because she doesn't want
them
to follow
in their father's footsteps

Oh Mama-bear
is going to lose again

The Praying Mantis

I saw
a praying mantis
this morning
you don't see
many of them
around anymore
these days

His hands
were clasped
his eyes were closed
and his head
was bowed
praying I suppose
without ceasing

Praying for forgiveness
praying for understanding
praying for patience
a little worried
about extinction
really worried
about how it happened
praying for strength
praying for guidance

praying for love
praying I suppose
without ceasing

I wonder if I'll ever see another praying mantis again
they are really rare these days

Amen

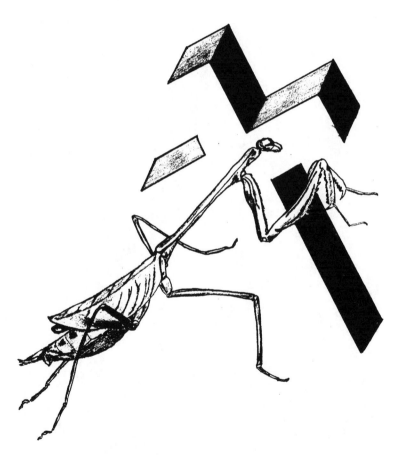

Praying Mantis,
a drawing by Steven Forris Kimbrough

ODES TO LOVE

A Laughing Matter

A fireman
president
a policeman perhaps

No said the child

Then what would
you like to be
when you grow up

In love
in love

Firemen
presidents
the whole world
laughed at once

Listen closely
they're still laughing

Blow a Kiss

Blow a kiss
as you're leaving
don't take your
camisole
down off the line
leave a footprint
in the garden
an impression
a sign

Then fly away
to your desire
and I will stay
near to the fire

Leave a message
on the mirror
using lipstick
as your pen
let your fragrance
fall on the pillow
I will catch it
now and then

Then fly away
to your desire
and I will stay
near to the fire

They say that
seeing is believing
but so many things
cannot be seen
so blow me a kiss
as you're leaving
I will see
what you mean

Orientation

To the time
with the oriental princess

She played
in water colors

I played the ch'in
We played
in love
and won

Entangled
intertwined
in love
indefinitely

She gave me
a thorough orientation

To the crime
against the oriental princess

He slayed
her
while I played
the ch'in
he slayed
in hate
and won

Strangled
interrupted
in love
instantly

She left me
thoroughly disoriented

Evolve in Love

Love without boundaries
is love that never dies
and love without condition
is love that never lies

Before the beginning
and after the end
only one thing remains
only love

Love without dominion
is love beyond control
and love without denial
is love beyond reproach

Before the beginning
and after the end
only one thing remains
only love

Love is always evolving
evolve, evolve in love
never stop falling
evolving in love

Even though It's Winter

This is beginning
to happen too often
we are saying good-bye again

I know when I will be back
and so do you
but what will we do till then

For a while
we have known the days
growing shorter
regardless

For a while
we have known the nights
even shorter
even though it's winter

For a while
we have known each other
but now it's ending
and this is beginning
to happen too often

Say It Not (Say I Love You)

I was once a flower
And if I'm ever
A flower again
I bet I'll
Stretch my petals
To the wind

And I was once an otter
And if I'm ever
An otter again
I will be playful
Spend my day-full
Summersaulting

Take this life
Take my hand
Be surprised
At all the love
You're unknowingly giving
Say it now
Say *je t'aime*
That's the only sound
The universe is hearing
Say
I will say never say die
I will live on
Don't think you can't fly
To the heavens
And please don't wait
For the morning dew
Say it now
Say I love you

I was once an archer
And if I'm ever
An archer again
I'll see my arrow
Meet the marrow
Of my friends

And I was once a lover
And if I'm ever
A lover again
I will gladly
Oh but sadly
See it end

Take Time to Love Someone

Take time to love someone
    take someone by the hand
if you take time to love
    then you will understand

How little time we have—
    don't squander it don't rove
take someone by the hand
    yes take the time to love

There's precious little time
    there's precious little touch
so little time for things
    that humans need so much

There's precious little joy
    there's precious little bliss
we need a flood-tide more
    of what we sorely miss

Waiting for the Morning

I was waiting for the morning
to bring the chance for me to say
I love you
I need you

But the morning never came
no chance left
for me to say
I love you
I need you

Lying peacefully there
do you hear
or wonder why I'm here
I came to say
I love you
I need you

I could have told you yesterday
I should have
but I was waiting for the morning
and it never dawned on me
till now

In Time for Love?

You missed our first rendezvous,
the table was set for two;
Sinatra was playing low,
but you decided—no show.

So you missed my sautéed veal,
it will be another meal;
on the table's other side,
watched the candle light subside.

Then I started off to bed,
thought twice—stuck around instead,
thinking maybe I was wrong,
thinking you might come along.

You came to the church on time,
flying rice, the wedding chime;
but I counted chicks too soon,
for you missed the honeymoon.

That was ages, years ago,
still there's something I don't know;
tell me please, how did you miss
the beauty of our first kiss.

Feel the Love

Open your eyes
    Open your heart
        Open your hands

And ... feel the love
And ... feel the love
And ... feel the love

Pouring in
    Pouring down
        Pouring out
            Of every pore

Opening flower
    Opening door
        Opening presence

And ... feel the love
And ... feel the love
And ... feel the love

Pouring in
    Pouring down
        Pouring out
            Of every pore

All Is Fair in Love

Down on my lunacy
the sun beats strong
even in my solitude
the mood plays along
naked in my silence
I wear a song
I wear a song

Sometimes my disability
has me all consumed
I feel like a flower cut
without the chance to bloom
but placed in your water
and I will fill the room
with a sweet perfume

The love we share
is O so rare
we know
all is fair in love
to have to hold
we break the mold
we know
all is fair in love

Shadows

When I die my love
my shadow will be waiting silently
on the other side
for you

But while I'm alive my love
beyond a shadow of a doubt
I'm going to find out
about loving you

We're just running for cover
living together
lover to lover
living forever
looking for that something
the Old Ones used to say
would make the shadows of the moon
meet the shadows of the day

Don't let the sadness in my eyes
hide the happiness I feel inside
my heart
for you

Don't let the kiss that's on my lips
fly off into the night
when it is meant
just for you

ODES TO THE "I"

There's More to You

I say
there's more to you
than meets
the I

You say
what gives you
such a crazy
idea

I say
it's all in the way
you look
at me

You don't say
anything
you just look
at me

I say
there's much more to you
than meets
the I

Eagle I

Eagle I
standing here
on the edge
of these very cliffs

Ready to take
that first leap
free-falling into flight
ready to cure
my fear of flying
for good
for once
for all

I have heard
the stories
of those
who have spread their wings
of those
who have spanned the ages

I have seen
others
take wing
and become as one
with the eternal formations

I have smelled
essential fragrances
my-way wafting
beckoning
luring
needing of response

I have felt
intense feelings
as I have learned
the harmonies
and melodies
of the Chorus of Experience

And now
as it challenges
here I stand
Eagle I
on the edge
of these very cliffs

Ready to take
my last leap
ready to open
my wings to the sun
in reverent adoration and praise
ready to assume
the spread-eagle
and stand before
the universe
and the very life forces themselves
in silent recognition
in humble gratitude
in everlasting anticipation

Eagle Flight,
a drawing by Steven Forris Kimbrough

I of the Storm

Covering the skies
like blankets of buffalo
across the plains
dark clouds gather
on the horizon
to count coup
one last time

I of the storm
rising swiftly now
Riding high
on the wings
of the thunderbird
Riding hard
lightning arrows
poised ready to fly

Dawn's first hues
leave me painted for battle
Wind in my hair
gusts of honor
gusts of pride
Heavy rains from my hands
beat down hard
in brave defense
Hail from heaven
wages holy warfare
riddles the unjust
with nature's own bullets

And I of the storm
rising swiftly now
Riding high

on the wings
of the thunderbird
Riding hard
lightning arrows
poised ready to fly
The winds may change
the winds may die
Then will the lightening
cease to strike
and the thunder
clap no more

And I of the storm
calm but not contented
silent but not silenced
forgiving but not forgotten
hardened but not heartless
tired of your peaces
tearing us to pieces
will find power in the stillness
forever still in power

Introspection

I looked me in the I
and saw

A man who needs goals
to give meaning
to life

A man who needs proof
to give meaning
to love

A man who needs academia
to give meaning
to truth

A man who needs gain
to give meaning
to expectation

A man who needs words
to give meaning
to silence

A man who needs progress
to give meaning
to nature

A man who needs boundaries
to give meaning
to freedom

A man who needs God
to give meaning
to everything

I couldn't believe my I

In the I of Modern Man

There is something in his I
is it a tear
that could be
since there's
a lot to cry about

There is something in his I
is it smoke
that could be
but most of it
is in his lungs

There is something in his I
is it a log
that could be
but he can't see
or feel it

There is something in his I
is it a light
that could be
but all it does
is blind him

There is something in his I
is it a look
that could be
but it's not love
I wish it was

ODES TO SELF

Confession

I did this
I did that
I knew I shouldn't
I never thought I would
I never thought I could
I didn't mean to

I tried to
I tried not to
I didn't
I should have
Should I have

I never did that before
I'm sorry
I won't ever do that again
I just don't know what came over me
I'm not like that

That's okay

I Am in a Sober Period Now

I am in a sober period now
and I am praying to stay
this way
I have smelled fresh morning air
I have tasted crystal mountain waters
I have felt a gentle breeze passing
I have seen children playing together
and in this moment
I have heard
the silence

And I am full of praise
for this silence
for this very stillness
which is now my sobriety
and for this crisp clean feeling
which is in my head
and in my heart
and in the very balls of my feet

Indeed
there is boundless praise inside me
for the reason for this emancipation
and if my mother be the reason
(and I think she is the reason)
then all praise and glory be to her
and if my father be the reason
then all praise and glory be to him
and if my brothers and sisters be the reason
then all praise and glory be to them
and if our Nature-Mother be the reason
(and I'm sure she is the reason)
then all praise and glory be to her

and if our God-Father be the reason
then all praise and glory be to him
and if you be the reason
then all praise and glory be to you
and if I be the reason
then all praise and glory be to me

For I am in a sober period now
full of love—full of life
and I am praying to stay
this way

Joy

Joy my mountain
sorrow my well
no heaven
without hell

Joy my mountain
sorrow my plain
no rainbow
without rain

Let it rain oh
let it rain
let it rain oh
let it rain

Joy my fountain
sorrow my well
time will tell

Polaroid Flashback

Make me think
of that picture
you gave me
what seems like years ago

An old faded Polaroid shot
of you
after you had
climbed a mountain
with some friends

You were twelve
maybe thirteen

S. S. O

There is someone
who doesn't laugh
at you
who looks
into your eyes
and smiles

The Power of Now

By the power of now
I have opened my senses
I have lowered my defenses
to live in present tenses
without any pretenses

The Funny Position

You put me in a funny position
but I don't think I mind it
in fact I think I like it

What you're doing right now
well that's so very nice
I am really feeling now
and you are smiling

This is all so brand new
and I'm not really sure
what to do
I've never been
in this position
and goodness
this is a funny position
but I don't mind it
I don't mind it at all

I closed the third volume of *The Cadillac Poems*. Some of them I had read earlier when Steven passed them along to me in a printed format. For others this was my first reading.

From where I sat at the moment in the large back room he had added to the old farmhouse, I could look directly into the woods, for the entire room was rimmed with vertical windows. Just as I glanced up from the closed volume, a cardinal perched gracefully on the ledge beyond the windows. A quatrain that Steven once penned and that is embedded in my memory came to mind.

By any other name
He is always the same
A spirit of the earth
A cardinal by birth.

The regal cardinal remained still and perched in its place for what seemed to be ten minutes or more. I was entranced by its solitude beyond the windowpane. Finally it fluttered its wings as if to bid me good-bye and flew off into the woods.

I looked around the room once more before I departed simply to breathe in Steven's space and that of his children. As I rose, my eyes fell on a compact disc nestled beneath the right side of his computer. Sliding it out gently, for it had no cover, to my surprise the inscription on it in Steven's handwriting was "The Poems of Steven Forris Kimbrough." Having spent so many hours with his words and thoughts, I could not resist pressing the on button of the computer and slipping the CD-R into the appropriate slot. It was an old computer and laboriously slow, and I became extremely impatient when the contents of the disk did not appear immediately on the screen. Slowly they emerged—more poems. As I scrolled through them, I found many from *The Cadillac Poems*. Others I had read before, but some I was seeing for the first time.

ODES TO FAITH

Jonah's Lamentation

Seeking safe harbor
sinking feeling
wanting only
to be moored
did you get the message
or just the bottle
empty washed up
on the shore

Your arms harbor me
wind and water at bay
your arms harbor me
out of harm's way

Seeking safe harbor
before I am lost
treading water
o'er my grave
you've pierced my armor
and I'm taking water
swallowed by one whale
of a wave

Your arms harbor me
wind and water at bay
your arms harbor me
out of harm's way

The light in your house
can I reach it
it's on
should the ocean spit me out
then I will hit the beach

hit the beach running—
running—
into your arms—

Your arms harbor me
wind and water at bay
your arms harbor me
out of harm's way

Forty Days and Forty Nights[3]
(based on Genesis 7)

Forty days and forty nights
    there's endless wind and rain;
forty days and forty nights
    you can see no terrain.
The sea surrounds the whole world,
    the winds display their might:
giant seas with waves unfurled;
    there is no land in sight.

Refrain:
So build a ship of love;
    weather the stormy sea,
riding the waves above
    each hardship that you see.
A little bird reveals
    that which you need to know.
God's loving memory
    is every rainbow.

3   Words © 2009 Steven F. Kimbrough. Administered by The General Board of Global Ministries, GBGMusik. All rights reserved. Used by permission.

Should the Spirit beckon you,
    you'd better heed the call;
into your hands a blueprint
    may happen then to fall,
filled with divine instruction,
    (survival guaranteed),
plans for the construction
    to float the ship you need.

Refrain

Gather in the gopher wood,
    make haste the clouds are thick;
build the ship in your backyard,
    each board by board, be quick.
All creatures that are living
    bring two by two on board.
There will be no misgiving
    that life will be restored.

The Greatest Song of All
(1 Corinthians 13)

1. In the womb we hear the rhythm
        of our mother's beating heart;
    in her arms she gently soothes us
        with her humming from the start.
    When she rocks the cradle slowly
        with the sounds of lullabies,
    we are magic'lly transported,
        as she quiets all our cries.

    Refrain:
    Sing a song of faith,
    sing a song of hope,

sing a song of love,
sing the greatest song of all, the song of love.

2. It seems that everything we learn
   from our childhood early·on
   is accompanied by music,
   is accompanied by song.
   Just listen and you will hear it,
   an unending melody,
   it's the music of the Spirit,
   it's a song of unity.

Refrain

3. They're sacred songs, they're secular,
   there are hymns and there are cheers;
   there is music all around us,
   there is music from the spheres;
   but mothers' first sung lullaby,
   we can never learn too soon
   for you're happiest when you're singing,
   when you've learned to sing love's tune.

Refrain:
Sing a song of faith,
sing a song of hope,
sing a song of love,
sing the greatest song of all.

Sing a song of peace,
sing a song of grace,
sing a song of love,
sing the greatest song of all, the song of love.

Prayer for Today

May today be a good day
  for my friends and for all
  my relations.
May I always remember to give
  thanks for living as I
  continue to grow in the
  goodness of mother earth.
May I stand in the silence
  that is all around
  hearing prayers unspoken
  remembering those who
  have gone before and
  those who are yet to
  come.
May I feel this day the power
  and presence of God;
May I pray with that presence
  as it prays with me.
May I walk the road of purity
  surrounded by beauty,
  respectful of all things.
Always empowered to listen
  forever strengthened by
  thanksgiving, eternally
  sustained by silence,
  remembering to give back
  to the earth what is hers.
Keeping it simple, spontaneous,
  receiving all, holding none,
May I help someone
  and learn something new today.

I Am Me

I am me
I am myself
and I am I.
I am here to live
and here to die

I am me
I am an artwork
of God's hands
and yet our hands
hung and bled him.

I am different
I am proud
I am odd
still I am the handiwork
of God.

I know it's hard
to comprehend
so please do not try,
because it's just me,
and myself,
that's why I am I.

Christmas Today

In not just one way
was it Christmas today
it was the cards
it was the letters
it was the ornaments

Yes some spirit is working
and so are we
yes some spirit is playing
and so are we

And now as I sit here
full of cheer
I could not but think
what Jesus would say—
Christmas is not one birthday
once a year
Christmas is today
and every other day

Roses in December[4]

This year there are roses in December
blossoming the day the Lord is born,
and I believe I always will remember
the Birth — the Blood — the Rose — the Thorn
the Birth — the Blood — the Rose — the Thorn.

Snow is falling gently in the garden
blanketing the beds with cover deep.
As the longest night falls upon all,
the prayer is for the Lord all souls to keep.

This year there are roses in December
blossoming the day the Lord is born,
and I believe I always will remember
the Birth — the Blood — the Rose — the Thorn
the Birth — the Blood — the Rose — the Thorn.

So as the Sun eclipses the horizon,
dawn is breaking on this joyous day;
streaming light illuminates the garden
shining on a Rose seeming to say:
Love is born today,
Love is born today,
Love is born today,
the Birth — the Blood — the Rose — the Thorn
the Birth — the Blood — the Rose — the Thorn.

Alleluia, alleluia, alleluia,
alleluia!
Alleluia, alleluia, alleluia,
alleluia,

---

4   Steven's last poem written in December 2009.

the Birth — the Blood — the Rose — the Thorn
the Birth — the Blood — the Rose — the Thorn.

This year there are roses in December
blossoming the day the Lord is born,
and I believe I always will remember
the Birth — the Blood — the Rose — the Thorn
the Birth — the Blood — the Rose — the Thorn.

MISCELLANEOUS POEMS

Invisible Ink

Tipping the velvet
Tipping the pearl
Tiptoeing through tulips
Until your tiptoes
Curl

Tipping the balance
In favor of pink
Tipping the well over
Oops
Oh well
Spilling the ink
Invisible ink

Lucifera Serenades

Lost in translation
Deep in the word
Lost in salvation
No wonder
No one heard

Down through the ages
Between every line
Dripping from the pages
Chilling every spine

Lucifera serenades

Defying definition
Her blessing her disguise
Beyond recognition
Occulted lullabies

Lucifera Serenades

Rock-a-bye Baby
In the treetops
When the wind blows
The cradle will rock
When the bough breaks
Your skin starts to crawl
Then down from the heavens
The angel will fall

Off to Vegas

So you're flying off to Vegas
    Chips to blow and roll the dice;
While the children all must stay home,
    And they'll surely pay the price.

Cheating single, cheating married,
    Separate or by divorce,
White lies are an appetizer,
    Pure deceit the final course.

Driftwood

Driftwood
would drift
but the drifting days
are over

No more
lonely deserted beaches
no more
choppy seas
no more

sun and sand
now it's
fun on land

High tide is out
high life is in

Driftwood
as antiques
decorations
in boutiques
nature's sculptured
physiques
living room
uniques

Big time is here
little time is left

Because
driftwood
would drift
but the drifting days
are over

On Setting a World Record

They passed
almost like ships in the night
but they were oil tankers
so it didn't quite work
the way it usually does

Instead they crashed
like ships in the night
more than determined
to cause the world's
largest oil slick

And they got it too—
a new world record

Smile a Little Harder

Smile a little harder
and I think
the sun might rise
tomorrow—
it is good
to feel the sun
in your face

Smile a little harder
and the good earth
will sustain you
today—
it is good
to know the power
of the earth

Smile a little harder
and the people
will forget what happened
yesterday—
it's amazing
what a little smile
can do

Smile a little harder
open wide
like an endless summer's sky
forever—
it is good
to know the freedom
of a smile

The Best Friend (I Never Had)

Every time the phone rings
every time a bird sings
I hold my breath
and hope it's you
calling

And when I see a rainbow
I know I will never follow
my heart
a dream of you and me
falling

The moment we met
there was no doubt
now I must forget
bottle up these feelings
never let them out

Over before
it ever began
end of the story
never looking back
as you just turned
and ran

One moment so glad
the next so sad
I just lost the best friend
that I never had

The Flea Market

The young people
go to
the flea market
the first Saturday
of the month

They're looking
for good times
and good buys

But you never know
what you'll find
at the flea market

Maybe the past
maybe a present

The old people
go too
they're selling their
good times
saying good-byes

They know
they'll never find
the past at the flea market

But maybe the present

The Vegetarian Man

The vegetarian man
is very healthy
he eats lots of fruits
and nuts

He's not fanatical
just practical
about his lifestyle
no beef
no pork
no fowl

Occasionally
he eats fish
but he mainly sticks to
grains and vegetables

He loves papaya juice
and frequently boasts
about his high
fiber intake
I like the vegetarian man
he's so natural
he's so healthy
he's so open and honest
he's really together

Yoga and jogging are also
very important parts of
the vegetarian man's lifestyle
he used to jog passed my window every day

But he won't be jogging
anymore

Yesterday
he choked to death
on a piece of carrot

The Fix-It Man

There is a man they say
Down Carolina way
Who can see to it
If you can't screw it
To the wall
If someone blew it
In the hall
He won't nix your request
He'll just fix it the very best
That he can
He's affectionately known
And appropriately so
As the Fix-It Man

He can't repair your heart
But he's got any spare part
For your refrigerator
For your master generator
Down the stairs
For the AC turned heater
He's got spares
He won't nix your request
He'll just fix it the very best
That he can
He's affectionately known
And appropriately so

As the Fix-It Man

If you are in a fix
He'll do the best he can
His tricks they ain't for kids
He's the Fix-It Man

What good is Santa Claus
If you've a problem without a cause
He can fill your stockings
But can he stop electrical shockings
In your attic
Or inexplicable unlockings
Or TV static
He won't nix your request
He'll just fix it the very best
That he can
He's affectionately known
And appropriately so
As the Fix-It Man

There is a man they say
Down Carolina way
His specialty is shelves
He doesn't need elves
You must fix it for yourselves
The fact is
They always nix your requests
So you've got to fix it the very best
That you can
It's your only hope
If you want to cope
With the law of the land
Be a Fix-It Man

The Broom

Old and bent
just about worn out
after so many years
of being pushed around
by people
back and forth
forth and back
it's time to retire

Almost bald
ragged and filthy
after so many miles
of dirt and dust
only memories of
back and forth
forth and back
it's time to retire

Alone and lonely
closeted and forgotten
after so few praises
from so few people
just back and forth
forth and back
it's time to retire

Epilogue

It is early August 2010. It has taken almost eight months to renovate the old farmhouse since Steven's death. I am walking from room to room, inspecting all that has been done. The house is completely empty, freshly painted walls, floors waxed, new tile laid around the large bathtub. There is a smell of freshness, and Dakotah and Savannah will soon move back to the house with their mother for a new beginning.

Outside I stand pensively for a while by the pond at the place where some of Steven's ashes were reverently placed in the water by his brother Timothy.

I turn and walk across the lawn to check the sheds (the children's chalets) beside the house where many of their possessions and those of their father are stored. Everything is secure. Beside the shed nearest the road there are still a couple of deep ruts where the old Cadillac had stood for so long. It is gone for good, but *The Cadillac Poems* will be with us always.

Steven Forris Kimbrough
(1958–2010)

STEVEN FORRIS KIMBROUGH WAS born November 7, 1958 in Birmingham, Alabama. He began school in Princeton, New Jersey, and moved with his family to Germany when he was eleven years old. He attended both German and American schools in Bonn and excelled in his studies and athletics. After completion of High School, he entered Duke University, as did his brothers Timothy and Mark. With majors in German and Art Design, he graduated *magna cum laude* in 1980.

After graduation from Duke University, he became a resident of Cedar Grove, NC, where he lived until his death. Though he lost a leg as a youth, he learned to ski again and was a Cross Country Skiing medalist in the 1979 Handicap Olympic National Championships.

In 2010 Kimbrough died in an automobile accident. He was a gifted linguist, as his poems in English, German, and French illustrate, and an ardent supporter of Native American life and causes. He was also a talented artist, whose drawing of the fossil, *Aegyptopithecus,* a major link in the evolutionary chain, was published in the *New York Times, Time* Magazine, and *Newsweek.* His poem "Forty Days and Forty Nights" was set to music and published in the book of global songs and activities for children, *Put Your Arms Around the World.* Music was one of his passions and for about ten years he played bass guitar and wrote song lyrics in the group, *One Real Band,* with his brothers, Timothy and Mark, which became quite popular during their Duke University years.

His first love was family, especially his children, Dakotah and Savannah.

His poetry reflects a broad worldview and a keen sensitivity to nature, the marginalized, the physically challenged, one's view of self and others, and the need for faith and love in the world today.

S T Kⁱᵐᵇʳᵒᵘᵍʰ, Jʀ., compiler/editor of this volume, holds a
Ph.D. from Princeton Theological Seminary and is an interna-
tionally known scholar/musician who has published some forty
books and numerous articles on biblical, theological, historical,
liturgical, musical, poetical, literary, and Wesleyan subjects. He
has made numerous recordings on leading labels and performed
on radio/television networks and outstanding stages in the USA,
Europe, and Asia.